The tall ships
R 797.1 CLA

P9-DIZ-204

Clark, Hyla M.
Medway High School Library

The Tall Ships

A Sailing Celebration

TEXT BY HYLA M. CLARK
INTRODUCTIONS BY FRANK O. BRAYNARD
AND TONY GIBBS

PUBLISHED IN ASSOCIATION WITH
OPERATION SAIL 1976

For Reference

Not to be taken

from this library

A TREE C...............GORY BOOK

R
797.1
C

Created and
produced by Tree Communications, Inc.
250 Park Avenue South, New York, New York
Publisher: Bruce Michel
Editorial director: Rodney Friedman
Design director: Ronald Gross
Director of photography: Paul Levin
Art director: Sonja Douglas
Production: Lucille O'Brien
Design assistants: Christopher Jones, Patricia Lee
Research assistant: Elizabeth Henley

Copyright © 1976
Tree Communications, Inc./Helvetica Press, Inc.
All rights reserved.
No part of this work may be reproduced or trans-
mitted in any form by any means, electronic or
mechanical, including photocopying and recording,
or by any information storage or retrieval system,
without permission in writing from the copyright
holder.

Distributed by Two Continents, 30 East 42 Street,
New York, New York 10017
Printed and bound in the United States of America
First printing: November, 1976

Assisting in the production of this book:
Consulting editor: Tony Gibbs
Text editor: Nancy Naglin
Copyreaders: Laurence Barandes, Jerry Weinberg
Typesetter: Iris Rautenberg

Acknowledgements:
The author wishes to thank Abel Cruz of the South
Street Seaport Museum Book & Chart Store and
Norman Brouwer, the South Street Seaport Museum
Librarian.

Special mention:
Alexis Gregory and Janet Calvo for, independently,
spotting and pursuing an impossible book.

Photo and illustration credits:
David Arky, photo, page 106 (top)
R. Alan Bennington, photos, pages 62-63, 94 (top),
99
Jan Cobb (from The Image Bank), photo, pages 58-59
Craig Cooper, photos, pages 85, 88, 89, 101 (bottom)
Leo de Wys, Inc., photos, pages 70, 82-83, 95, 98,
108, 109
Sonja Douglas, maps, pages 78-79
Edward A. Foote (from Authenticated News Inter-
national), photo, pages 104-105
Lawrence Fried (from The Image Bank), photo,
page 74
Geoffrey Gove (from The Image Bank), photo, pages
110-111
Alexis Gregory, photos, pages 118, 122-23
Ted Hardin (from Black Star), photos, pages 68-69,
75
Jane's Fighting Ships, illustrations, page 64 (Reprint-
ed by permission of the publisher, © MacDonald &
Jane's, Ltd., London, from the 1972-73 edition,
page 438)
Christopher Jones, illustrations, pages 22 and 23
Paul Levin, photo, page 107
Steven Mays, photos, pages 28-29, 36-37, 46-47
Leighton Miller, photo, page 102
Larry Naar, photo, back cover
Tsuneo Nakamura, photos, pages 24, 25, 26, 27,
30-31, 32, 33, 38, 39, 40, 41, 42, 43, 49, 50, 51, 52, 53,
54, 55, 56, 57, 71, 84 (Reprinted by permission of the
photographer from *The Sailing Ships of the World*, ©
1976 by Heibonsha, Tokyo)
The New York *Daily News*, photos, pages 60, 61,
80-81, 90-91, 100, 106 (bottom), 116 (bottom),
117, 119
Operation Sail 1976, photo, page 48
Gabe Palmer (from The Image Bank), photo, page
128
Darleen Rubin, photos, pages 94 (bottom), 96-97
Anita Sabarese (from D.P.I.), photos, pages 120, 121
The Sailing Ships of the World, illustration, pages
20-21 (Reprinted from pages 82-83 by permission of
the publisher, © 1976 by Heibonsha, Tokyo)
K. Scholz (from Shostal Associates), photo, front cover
Eric Schweikardt (from The Image Bank), photo,
pages 45, 92-93
Shostal Associates, photos, pages 34-35, 44, 72-73,
76-77, 86-87, 112
Max Tortel (from D.P.I.), photo, page 101 (top)
Wide World Photos, photos, pages 72-73, 103, 116
(top), 126-27

The text face for this book is Plantin, set at Tree Communications, Inc. The display type is Franklin Gothic,
set at Latent Lettering Co., Inc. Original color separa-
tions were made by National Colorgraphics, Inc. Half-
tones were made by International Plate Service Corp.
The papers used are 80 lb. Warren Flokote, supplied
by the Lindenmeyr Paper Corporation, and 70 lb.
Miami Book, supplied by the Baldwin Paper Company. The book was printed and bound by Connecticut Printers Incorporated.

Clark, Hyla.
    The tall ships.

    "A Tree Communications / Alexis Gregory edition."
    1. Operation Sail 1976.   2. Sailing ships.
3. American Revolution Bicentennial, 1776-1976 – New
York (City)   I. Title
VK543.C57 1976   797.1'4'091631   76-43112
ISBN 0-8467-0236-3
ISBN 0-8467-0237-1 pbk.

MEDWAY HIGH SCHOOL LIBRARY

Book No. 13,716

t happened and amazed everyone. For those of us who had the double fun of working on it from the beginning, Operation Sail was a tremendous experience and a wonderful fulfillment. And watching the event brought such spectacular joy to all of us—how can it ever be relayed to the future?

A book about *Operation Sail 1976* can only skim over the whole picture. No one can ever capture, let alone put on paper, the thrill of the five-year build-up and the sense of satisfaction as piece after piece fell into place. Who could possibly relive those exciting preliminaries: the marvelous Operation Sail at Kiel, West Germany, where for the first time the *Wilhelm Peck*, an East German ship, participated and won the race; or the grand review at Cowes, England, in 1974, where both *Kruzenshtern* and *Tovaristsch* passed before Prince Philip aboard the sleek *Britannia*.

And how can we put into words Operation Sail's growth from the Bicentennial's "best kept secret," which is what it was for four and a half years, to the number one event of the Bicentennial? How can we record its growth, which was slow and hectic with many stumbling blocks? Many prize ships of Operation Sail refused to participate when first invited. In virtually every case, negotiations began with a negative response, and in several instances, changing minds took as long as two years and involved thousands of letters. But it was surely worth it.

To have 16 of the available 20 Tall Ships take part was something to be proud of. And to have some 50 medium-sized tall ships was another contribution to the color and impact of Operation Sail, not to mention the assortment of more than 100 smaller sailing vessels, classic yachts and other historic craft. We were proud of each and every one of them, particularly the 62 sailing yachts from Hamburg, Germany, whose expedition here overcame so many difficulties. And we were proud of the *Leifur Eriksson* from Iceland and the *Sebbe Als* from Denmark, the two Viking ship replicas that made it, as well as the nine outstanding Dutch sailing yachts transported on board container ships. Those nine beauties, together with the Netherlands' sail-training schooner *Eendracht*, stretched the impact of Operation Sail all the way up to Albany and extended the wonder and thrill of the event to millions who did not see the ships in New York.

And what marvelous people we will remember—what faces, what charming accents, what happy voices, and what grand seamen. For that whole week every street corner, every waterfront, every nook and cranny of our port was filled with white-uniformed seamen, and the tales of the hospitality afforded to them are untold. New York arose to welcome them, to embrace them, to thank them for coming to our Birthday Party. The grand thing about it all was that their reception was just what you would want it to be, not tarnished by smallness or meanness of any kind. New Yorkers welcomed them and they sailed away, touched by the friendship of Americans.

This book is a picture book, but still we cannot offer the greatest picture of all. That is the picture of a city turned around and a state and nation renewed. It is the picture of the effect of Operation Sail on a whole country. This big picture awaits the big artist, the brush of a future Rembrandt, the text of a future Homer. Bear with us. We offer you an introduction to the excitement of *Operation Sail 1976*. Enjoy it and assist us in carrying the message of the event: The oceans do not divide us, they unite us all. We are all seamen on spaceship Earth.

Frank O. Braynard

FRANK O. BRAYNARD
GENERAL MANAGER, *OPERATION SAIL 1976*

Eight of us came down from Long Island Sound to New York Harbor on July 3, our boat dropping anonymously into the incredible mass of southbound vessels that squeezed under the Throgs Neck Bridge, shouldered their way through rainshowers past La Guardia airport, and at last emerged from under the Triboro into the East River proper—Manhattan straight ahead.

The first thing one sees, coming south through Hell Gate, is Gracie Mansion, the home of the mayors of New York with its private view of the river. On that day, the elegant lawn was all but obscured by people—the first example of what was to be the keynote of the weekend. Having made the East River passage both ways on many occasions, I was prepared for the architecture, but not for the humanity. There were heads in every window and people lining the Manhattan shore anywhere they could find standing room. From the elegant and costly riverside apartments, the inhabitants had hung flags and banners, echoing the pennants aboard the fleet that now swept, the full tide at its back, downstream.

Alongside us, with a steel band on the foredeck whanging away, was the Antiguan schooner *Free Lance*, and just ahead, the odd profile of a yacht whose round bows had bashed through the North Sea rollers. There had been rain squalls, and there were obviously more to come, but it made no difference to the watchers ashore, who cheered the fleet on with rousing generosity—and we among them, celebrants and celebrated, simultaneously going into port.

That evening we anchored in the Hudson, across from the bleachers at Battery Park City, among the largest fleet of pleasure craft I have ever seen. The river runs fast past Manhattan, and there was enough force in the three-knot ebb to pluck anchors from the bottom and whirl sail and power yachts into some fairly abrupt embraces. Surprisingly, few people seemed ruffled, clearly everyone so badly wanted the event to be a success, that from the moment of

dawn on July Fourth, success was assured.

We in the spectator fleet waited and ate, got our own flags up, and waited some more. Directly across from us, two Israeli gunboats were suddenly wreathed in smoke, the sound of the salute echoing seconds later. It had begun—to the south, under the Verrazano Bridge, we could see the U.S. Coast Guard bark, *Eagle*, glittering white in the water and aeons away from her origins as Hitler's training ship, *Horst Wessel*.

One by one the great ships came up the river, huge and silent and beautiful. Each one different and memorable—the delicately perfect ship-rigged *Danmark*; *Juan Sebastian de Elcano*, repaired after her Bermuda collision; the Russian *Kruzenshtern*, most militant-appearing of the fleet; Italy's magnificent *Amerigo Vespucci*, reminiscent of a high-sided refugee from Nelson's Trafalgar.

The spectacle was more than anyone could have imagined, but it never became excessive—due in part to yet another squall that cooled off the afternoon and put an emphatic (and slightly premature) end to the parade.

Monday morning, July 5, was ghostly quiet on the water. Most of the boats had left in the night after the fireworks. It was like the day following any huge party, but without the hangover. We motored back up the East River against the current. We felt subdued, somehow, but there was none of that empty feeling that so often follows a public event. On our boat and, I think, on the others chugging north with us, we felt like small but genuine participants in a piece of history. Less visible than the Tall Ships, we had still taken part. We had been touched by that great outpouring, that unique sense of communal celebration. We had been there and what we had seen still filled our hearts.

TONY GIBBS
ASSOCIATE EDITOR, *YACHTING MAGAZINE*

The Romance of the Sea

The 200th anniversary of the signing of the Declaration of Independence was a day of celebration throughout the United States. Every state had its Bicentennial commission, and communities all over the country tried to find some connection with the past.

New York City's giant "Salute '76" was particularly noteworthy. The city's festival featured Operation Sail 1976 – a great parade of sailing ships up the Hudson River. Some 225 international sailing vessels moved through two columns of 53 stationary warships which were participating in a simultaneous International Naval Review. The fleet of sailing ships featured 16 of the world's largest sailing vessels, colorfully known as "Tall Ships." The giant Russian bark *Kruzenshtern*, with a length of 375 feet 6 inches was the longest ship in the parade; the smallest was the *Gazela Primeiro*, originally a Portuguese fishing boat, 177 feet 10 inches long, now owned by the Philadelphia Maritime Museum. The rest ranged from about 250 to 300 feet in length.

The wonderfully apt phrase Tall Ship is a poetic reference originally penned by the late John Masefield, England's Poet Laureate. (Masefield was a sailor and had been a cadet aboard the British schoolship *Conway*.) Ships are generally classified in terms of tonnage, displacement or length, not in terms of height. But the height of a sailing ship's masts is a function of her size and weight, and the largest ships also tend to be the tallest. For the purposes of Operation Sail a Tall Ship was one that could not sail beneath the 125-foot Brooklyn Bridge.

Sailing buffs were euphoric at the sight of so many majestic ships, and landlubbers who jammed the city's shores were equally entranced. Those who stayed away, either fearing the crowds or citing commercialism, may have felt they had missed a once-in-a-lifetime event.

It was fitting that such a seafaring event should take place in New York Harbor. Most Manhattanites probably forget they live on an island in one of the greatest port cities in the world. Yet, the things which make New York City larger-than-life – the array of enterprises, the goods and services available beyond measure, even the rapid-fire pace, are all a direct result of New York's supremacy as a port.

In 1776, New Yorkers didn't know about the signing of the Declaration until July 9. As soon as they heard the good news, a group of patriots sliced off the head of a statue of George III. George III probably didn't hear about the colonies' independence until at least a month later – even a fast packet ship sailing from New York 50 years later needed 25 days to make the crossing. (The term "packet" refers to a ship that carries cargo and passengers on a regular basis. They may be either steam or canvas powered.)

The sailing packet ships of the 19th century had a great deal to do with shaping New York's future as a commercial giant. Without the great sailing ships, New York would not be what it is today. And without New York, the history of sailing would be missing a sizable chapter. In fact, some of the finest clipper ships in the world were constructed in the great East River shipyards.

The ships which travelled up the Hudson River on July 4, 1976, represent the modern remnants of a great sailing tradition. But it should be remembered that the Tall Ships taking part in Operation Sail 1976 were not relics restored from the past. Two – the *Libertad* from Argentina and the *Gloria* from Colombia – were built in the 1960s. All the rest, with the exception of the wooden ship *Gazela Primeiro*, built in 1883, are 20th century steel sailing ships.

The Russian ship *Kruzenshtern* made her last commercial voyage as the *Padua* in 1956. Many of the others were built as schoolships to train the world's navies and merchant sailors in the craft of seamanship.

The history of great sailing ships predates the American fight for independence by many years. Sailing ships had their earliest beginnings in various primitive vessels which prevailed (and are still in use) throughout the world. For more than 10,000 years wooden rafts, reed and wicker boats, dugout canoes and hide boats have all navigated the world's waterways with some success.

Some of the earliest historical evidence we have of ships comes from the Egyptians who constructed river craft for the Nile. Changes in ship construction developed very slowly. By 2000 B.C., the people of Crete were producing two kinds of ships—long boats designed for fighting and round ships for use as merchantmen.

The people who later became the Greeks overran the Cretans in 1000 B.C. Later, the Greeks who had settled Carthage were in turn conquered by the Phoenicians. Very little is known of either Greek or Phoenician vessels. Galleys were the fighting ships of the day, but ship scholars are hard put to decipher the actual arrangements of oars and oarsmen.

Of course sea power meant world power. After the Carthaginians had ousted the Greeks, they, in turn, had to contend with the Romans. In 300 B.C. the Punic Wars began to determine which of the two powers was to have supremacy. The Romans were not sailors but they were formidable military tacticians and quickly bested their seafaring opponents.

After establishing themselves as the rulers of their southern seas, the Romans began to move northward. There they encountered peoples, primitive by Roman standards but well-versed in the art of shipbuilding. Both the Vikings and the early Celtic peoples built strong and well-designed boats able to withstand the hazardous northern waters. At one time it was thought the Vikings had learned ship construction from the Romans, but their construction techniques reflect centuries of experimentation.

The Viking double-ended, single-masted style of ship construction persisted through the 13th century. During the next 200 years several important modifications took place. First, the side rudder evolved into a midships rudder attached to the sternpost, and the stern became flat. At the same time, shipbuilders began to realize that a deep-draft hull—a hull that extends into the water for a comparatively long distance—provides faster sailing closer to the wind. To take full advantage of this kind of hull, sails were made to set better against the wind. The forward edges of the square sail, which had previously flapped in the wind, were extended with bowlines. Since the bow was too close to the sail to secure it, a bowsprit, extending in front of the ship, developed. The bowlines ran through pulleys on the bowsprit and back to the main body of the ship.

Northern ships continued with a single square sail until the 15th century, but southern countries developed a different type of sail. Mediterranean ships carried lateen sails. The lateen is a triangular fore-and-aft sail, which

sets parallel to the keel of the ship; a square sail sets perpendicular to the keel. It is not known exactly where the lateen developed, but it is thought to have originated in Arabia. Lateen sails were particularly suited to the placid waters and variable breezes of the Mediterranean. But square sails offered greater sail area for long-distance runs before steady winds and worked much better in the harsher northern oceans. After becoming familiar with northern square sails, southern shipbuilders, particularly the Spanish and the Portuguese, began to adopt square sails.

Tremendous developments in sailing-ship design took place during the first 50 years of the 15th century. Unfortunately, little is known about the process. Almost overnight sailing ships changed from one mast and one sail to three masts and five or six sails. Soon many ships were built as full-rigged ships, which means they carried square sails on all their masts. And with the arrival of these ships, the age of exploration began.

Exploring ships were constrained by size limitations. A ship could not be too small or she would probably be destroyed in a heavy sea. On the other hand, an overly large ship would sacrifice crucial maneuverability needed in uncharted waters.

By the 16th century ships were becoming truly seaworthy. They were able to stay at sea

for months at a time. And as new discoveries provided an incentive for better ships, the improvements resulted in still more daring explorations.

Nations may have been at war at sea, but composite crews from rival sea powers manned explorer ships. In 1524, for example, the Italian Giovanni da Verrazano, sailing a French ship, discovered New York Harbor. Henry Hudson, an Englishman sailing for the Dutch government, discovered the Hudson River in 1607. A few years later the Dutchman Adriaen Block, sailing in one of his country's ships, landed at what is now lower Manhattan in order to trade with the Indians. When his ship burned, he was forced to set ashore in order to build another craft. Soon after, the Dutch West India Company obtained the rights to the land between the Delaware and Hudson Rivers, and in 1613 set up the permanent settlement of New Amsterdam.

By the early 17th century settlements had begun to dot the Atlantic coast. Jamestown was established in 1607, and in 1620, the Pilgrims established the Massachusetts Bay Colony at Plymouth, Massachusetts. In 1640, Swedes settled in what is now Philadelphia, and Charleston was established in 1670.

During the 18th century, the colonial port cities of the northeast established themselves as commercial centers. By pre-revolutionary times, Charleston, Boston, New York and Philadelphia were rivals in port size. Close to large forests, the New England colonies were immediately successful in shipbuilding. In the early 18th century shipbuilding flourished in the Delaware yards. Philadelphia had access to the great agricultural interior of Pennsylvania and traded grain to the southern colonies, and grain and iron to the northern ones. Charleston, separated from them by long distances and dangerous Cape Hatteras, developed differently. The southern port city became heavily involved in the West Indies trade. Ships sailed from Charleston loaded with indigo and rice. These cargoes were exchanged for sugar and rum, which in turn were traded to England for manufactured goods.

Commerce was lively, and by the second half of the 18th century, the North American colonies were thriving. Their prosperity made them increasingly attractive to British commercial interests. It also made the colonial bid for independence credible. Newly developed American wealth helped sustain the patriots through the long war that was to come, and the British decision to fight it on land may have given the colonists the tactical advantage.

As early as 1775, Lord Barrington argued that a successful blockade of the Atlantic coast could defeat the colonists. Barrington reasoned that commercial strangulation, with little loss of life or property, would force a quick reconciliation. But the Earl of Sandwich, First Lord of the Admiralty and Barrington's superior, believed the British army could easily defeat the rebel forces. After all, Great Britain had four times the colonial population, and barely half the colonists could be considered firm patriots.

But the Americans had much less trouble raising an army than the British. While outrage grew in the colonies, the war became increasingly unpopular in England. Colonial troops were rarely outnumbered in battle. Further-

more, American forces were able to recuperate in their own territory. The British troops were scattered in unfamiliar, often hostile places, and separated from their bases.

Meanwhile, the brand new American navy was doing a fine job of harassing the British merchant marine. Then in 1777, General Burgoyne surrendered after the Battle of Saratoga, and the French entered the conflict on the American side. At this point, the Revolutionary War evolved from an American bid for independence into an international naval war fought, in the main, for control of the valuable West Indian trade.

In early 1778, a French fleet sailed across the Atlantic. The main body of ships stayed in the West Indies, but a squadron and a small army made their headquarters in Newport, Rhode Island. The nearness of this fleet alarmed the British, who feared joint attacks of French and American forces. Under the unaggressive leadership of Sir Henry Clinton, commander in chief of the British forces in America, the British settled into a war of endurance.

Then in 1781, Lord Cornwallis attacked Yorktown, Virginia, with his entire force. The French fleet, under the command of Admiral de Grasse, sailed from the West Indies, and was met at Yorktown by General George Washing-

ton and his army, along with the French forces from Newport. Cornwallis found himself outnumbered and surrendered. Great Britain considered the battle decisive, and an Anglo-American treaty was signed on October 19, 1781.

The Revolution affected commerce in all American port cities, but New York's experience was unique. After the Battle of Long Island in 1776, the British occupied the city. Normal commercial flow was completely disrupted. The city was totally cut off from the surrounding countryside and forced to look to European markets for food.

Boston enjoyed a better position during the war, but peacetime British restrictions on the West Indies trade seriously interrupted New England commerce. Charleston never recovered her pre-revolutionary status. All in all, Philadelphia emerged from the Revolution as the strongest port city and for 13 years enjoyed commercial supremacy.

As the 19th century opened, all three northern ports seemed potentially able to dominate the eastern seaboard. Philadelphia had access to the fertile farmlands of Pennsylvania. Although New York only opened to the narrow Hudson River Valley, the river worked to the city's advantage by bringing upstate trade into the port. The outbreak of war between France and England in 1793 effectively removed British trade restrictions in the West Indies, and Boston was once again the center of thriving New England commerce. The Port of New York enjoyed many natural graces—a sheltered harbor with two approaches from the sea, a deep harbor and ample room for expansion—but not until the years following the War of 1812 did the city begin to realize its full potential.

The early years of the conflict between Great Britain and Napoleonic France were beneficial to American interests. American merchants not only traded with both sides, but assumed some of the trade previously controlled by both warring countries. But in 1807, the British and the French blockaded each other, and created an impossible situation for American ships: the French wanted to prohibit trade with or through England, and the British insisted that there be no trade *except* with England. Congress passed an embargo act in 1807, which closed all United States ports to foreign commerce, but the embargo was even more disastrous than attacks by belligerents.

The British further harassed the United States by stopping American ships and removing any English sailors on board. This was in direct conflict with the American concept of naturalization, but in keeping with the British idea of indelible allegiance. Not too wisely, in the early summer of 1812, the United States declared war on Great Britain. The United States had little hope of victory. This time the English fleet successfully blockaded the entire Atlantic coast.

American frigates and sloops of war did well enough against British vessels of similar ratings, and fast-moving privateers were developed to run the blockade. But by the end of the war, most American ships were shut up in port. For years ships sat idle in the yards of New York, Boston and Philadelphia. Finally, in late 1814, the United States and Great Britain began peace negotiations.

American forces had won a few battles against the British. However, Napoleon had been captured, the first Paris Peace Treaty had been signed, and American commerce was at a standstill. The United States was hardly in a commanding position, but the terms of peace were irrelevant. When news of the Treaty of Ghent reached New York in early 1815, the city's residents flocked into the snow-covered streets in the middle of the night to form an impromptu candlelight parade. Their jubilation would have been even greater if they could have known the century of growth that was yet to come.

The 19th century saw a completely new era in the history of shipbuilding and commerce. The aftermath of war brought a desire for speed. In the following decades canals and railroads were built. Steamships were invented, as well as ships made from iron, and then steel. Assisted by the expertise of earlier inventors, Robert Fulton built the first successful steamships.

Steamships were navigating bays and inland waterways, but sailing ships still controlled the oceans. Faster, more reliable ships and the confirmed regularity of the steamship lines gave Jeremiah Thompson the idea of running a sailing packet line from New York to Liverpool on a regular basis. His famous "Black Ball" line paid handsomely. The four Black Ball packets coming into port three times a year brought

more cargo than the heavily loaded East India ships which arrived only once a year.

But growing demand for speed and regularity signaled the decline of the sailing packet liners. Steamships could make the same offer and then some. In 1838, the *Sirus* and the *Great Western* were the first steamships to sail from London. The *Sirus* made the crossing in 19 days and the *Great Western* in 14½. The Black Ball packets took 25 days.

In the early days of steam, disasters were not uncommon and passengers were understandably leery. But the British government was so enthusiastic about the success of the *Sirus* and the *Great Western*, it requested bids for a mail service between Liverpool and the United States. Samuel Cunard received the contract. With the help of substantial government subsidies, he created the famous Cunard steamship line. By 1840, regular routes to Boston were established. (Boston triumphed briefly over her rival to the south. But eight years later the Cunard Line moved to New York.)

The Cunard Line offered speed and reliability and had an excellent safety record. Sailing packets could not hope to compete and soon became obsolete. However, sailing ships could compete with power vessels over longer distances. Fast sailing ships still had commercial potential. Under the growing pressure of steam, the racehorses of the sailing ships—the famed clipper ships—developed from design principles used in the sailing packets and in the Baltimore clipper schooners. The wooden clipper ships flourished briefly in the middle of the 19th century; then they were forever replaced by steam and steel.

The clipper ship has been variously defined. Generally it was a ship with a narrow elongated bow and a rounded stern. The clippers were not designed for cargo but for speed. The masts were high and the sails were numerous. As a result, the highly complicated ships required larger crews than standard ships. They were expensive to build and expensive to run—thoroughbreds in all respects.

The selling point of the clipper was speed. Her trade was expensive, and only the finest cargoes and wealthiest passengers could afford her rates. Speed was essential in the China tea trade—the fragile herbs would spoil quickly in the hull of a slow-sailing ship. Then in 1848, gold was discovered in California, and there was a frantic race to reach the gold fields.

any clipper ships were built in the New York East River yards. In fact, from 1840 to 1860, one East River shipbuilder, William Webb, produced more ships in his firm than any other American shipbuilder. He built packets and steamships as well as clippers, and clipper ships were always constructed from the finest materials. Live oak was shipped from Florida. Lighter locust and red cedar were used for decks and upper timbers, and the ships were outfitted with magnificent cotton sails. Cost was no object. Only the steadily increasing business of the Port of New York could support such expensive ships.

Most New York shipbuilders did their own design work until the end of the 1830s. The fol-lowing decade produced the naval architect. Outstanding in the field was John Willis Griffiths whose innovative design was first used for the China clipper *Rainbow*. Griffiths and two other giants, William Webb and Donald McKay, were the masters of the clipper-ship era. Webb turned out ship after ship of high quality (his firm once launched a packet, a steamship and a clipper all on the same day). One of his best ships was the *Challenger*, built expressly for the Gold Rush. Griffiths was the innovator and unsurpassed theoretician of the clipper ship. His great *Sea Witch* is said to have broken more speed records than any other American clipper. McKay was the inspired builder, and his *Flying Cloud* is considered by some to be the finest clipper ever built.

England was indignant to discover that a Yankee clipper could sail from New York to San Francisco, continue to China with only ballast, and still compete with the English tea

ships. Consequently Britain developed her own clipper ships. The *Cutty Sark* is probably the most famous of all English clipper ships. But by the time she was built in 1869, an iron clipper ship had already been built. The *Cutty Sark* was a composite construction—her frame was iron and her deck and hull were wood. The firm of Scott and Linton went out of business building the *Cutty Sark* but they constructed a beautiful hull.

The clipper ships worked the China tea trade, the Australian grain trade and the California Gold Rush. Clippers sailed from London around Cape Horn to China and back again loaded with tea. They rushed to Melbourne in 60 days through the same route.

Stories of clippers racing for tea and grain are some of the most romantic tales in the annals of sailing. Sailing around the cape was often a brush with death. At the bottom of the earth, winds create waves which circle the globe without striking land. Ships were further endangered by ice. The helmsman might have to be lashed to the wheel to prevent him from being swept overboard when a 40- or 50-foot wave washed over the stern. Sometimes a whole watch—half the crew—might be washed overboard. Square-rigged vessels were built to absorb the stress of the wind behind the masts, not in front of them. If the wind came around in front, the masts might be blown down. The sea could stave in a ship's hatches and put her under. And if she made it around the cape, she might lose buoyancy forward and simply sail under the sea.

Despite the speed, the excitement and the romance, clippers were racing to their extinction. In 1869, the Suez Canal was completed, and the steamship route to China opened up. Steamships using the canal whittled a full month off the clippers' time. The rumor circulated that tea was ruined in an iron hull and that the fumes from a steam engine affected its taste. But soon no one remembered the taste of China tea transported in a wooden hull.

The California Gold Rush trade also couldn't last. Like the British, the United States subsidized a mail route to San Francisco, and the Pacific Mail Steamship Company immediately came into being. Steamships sailed from New York to Panama. Cargo and passengers were transported by rail, mule and steamship across the isthmus and picked up on the other side by steamship. There was danger from malarial fever and the trip was uncomfortable. But the route across the isthmus avoided the perils of the cape and a month was sliced off the passage.

The only profitable routes left for a sailing ship were the Chilean nitrate trade and the Australian wool and grain trade. Some clipper ships moved into the wool and grain trade, the *Cutty Sark* among them (for a time she even hauled case oil), but these areas were dominated by the last of the great commercial sailing vessels, the Flying "P" line of steel ships, built by the Laeisz House in Germany at the end of the 19th and the beginning of the 20th centuries. These

enormous steel sailing ships were often ten times the size of the clippers and fully as romantic and glamorous as their famous predecessors.

The Laeisz family had been in the shipping business since before 1800. They began constructing wooden sailing ships in 1839, and by the 1880s were building great steel vessels designed exclusively for the nitrate trade. A wooden ship could not have been constructed on the same scale as the great Laeisz steel ships. Wood is a flexible material and begins to give when a ship is built too large. In a steel or an iron ship, the keel and the decks are equally strong. Iron had virtually replaced wood and composite construction by the 1870s, and by the 1880s steel had replaced iron. Ships increased steadily in size and strength, and the advent of steel rigging further increased their potential. The Laeisz ships were equipped to sail in gale force winds; the six-story waves off Cape Horn endangered the crew, but not the vessel. None of the Laeisz steel ships ever disappeared rounding Cape Horn.

The Laeisz House first built the four-masted ships *Pisagua* and *Placilla*. The *Placilla* could sail from England to Chile in just 60 days. Then they built the great ship *Preussen*, possibly the greatest sailing ship of all time. She was an enormous five-masted steel ship, 433 feet long, and capable of carrying 8,000 tons of cargo. Yet she needed only a 47-man crew.

But even these great ships were doomed. With World War I the bottom dropped out of the business. The sailing ships became prohibitively expensive to build and maintain. Chemical plants capable of producing nitrates were developed, and the trade with Chile fell off. Finally the Panama Canal was completed. A steamship could easily pass through the canal, but a sailing ship could not navigate the entranceway. Most of the Laeisz ships were out of service by the beginning of World War II. The grain trade was the last hope, and it was a slim and declining market. The last working Laeisz ship, the *Passat*, retired from the grain trade in 1956.

No more commercial sailing vessels have been built since the Flying "P" line. However, steel sail-training vessels have been built as late as the 1960s. A sizable fleet of schoolships remains scattered around the world — although few cadets will ever work a sailing ship. In a sailing ship a cadet works in close contact with the sea; the pilot of an engine-powered ship sometimes cannot even see the water beneath him. In a sailing ship the human element is crucial, and the experience therefore highly beneficial.

Of course, training under sail is nothing new. Apprentices have been going to sea on sailing ships practically as long as sailing ships have existed. Families often paid to have their sons learn the lore of the sea. Boys as young as 12 or 13 were taken to sea and raised on board ship.

Ships which function entirely as schools — boarding schools under sail — are a relatively recent phenomenon. The Swedish were the first to set up a merchant schoolship in the mid-19th century. Scandinavian merchants have traditionally trained boys under sail. Their benevolent training organizations work both for the future of the boys and the merchants' own well-being, for well-trained captains make prosperous ships.

The Norwegian Christiania Schoolship Association is representative of the Scandinavian system. In 1877, a citizens' group founded the sail-training organization for boys of poor circumstances. The school was first operated in a stationary ship during the summer months because the organization had difficulty raising the capital to purchase a seaworthy, deep-water vessel. In 1915 a wealthy merchant, Christian Radich, awarded the school an endowment with which to purchase a ship, provided that the ship and all its successors bore his name. The *Christian Radich* in the 1976 Operation Sail is the namesake of that first ship. Today, the organization is still without government support and operates solely on contributions.

In the late 19th century, the United States Congress passed a bill to subsidize sail-training schools in individual states. New York State was the first to make use of the funds to set up a sail-training school in 1875. Several New England states followed suit, but only Massachusetts still operates a school under the original mandate. However, under new legislation there are now sail-training schools in Maine, Texas and California.

At first the British were completely opposed to sail training. They argued that power-vessel crews would not accept a sail-trained officer. They feared class rivalries resulting from the officers' specialized sail training. By the 1950s they had reversed their opinion, and today there are a half dozen sail-training associations in Great Britain. Many of the English schoolships are open to young people regardless of their background or future plans. The English believe that character building is a general advantage gained on a sailing ship. They also don't require that the boys be boys — the *Sir Winston Churchill* joined Operation Sail with a cadet crew composed entirely of young women.

Sometimes a sailing ship no longer in service is used as a stationary schoolship or converted to a floating museum. For example, the *Cutty Sark*, the last clipper ship in the world, survives as a museum ship. She is cared for by the *Cutty Sark* Preservation Society in England.

Oceanography schools also have become interested in schoolships, but naval training accounts for most of the sailing ships afloat today. The United States Coast Guard is delighted with the crews trained on the *Eagle*, and many other nations are similarly pleased with their government-owned sail-training ships. Russia is thought to have the biggest fleet of schoolships, but figures have never been verified. She sent two ships to Operation Sail. One of them, the *Kruzenshtern*, was formerly the *Padua* of the Laeisz Flying "P" line. As she sailed up the Hudson, the Russian vessel passed not far from her sister ship the *Peking*, now owned by the South Street Seaport Museum and docked at the South Street pier.

The Ships
Tall ships, small ships, naval ships

The arrival of the tall sailing ships in New York Harbor was one of the most publicized events of the National Bicentennial festival. Understandably, the photogenic Tall Ships, differentiated from other visiting vessels primarily by their inability to pass under the 127-foot Brooklyn Bridge, got most of the glory. But they were only the most noticeable part of a vast sea parade several years in the making and were substantially outnumbered by over 200 smaller training vessels, 53 somber warships and thousands of enthusiastic pleasure boats.

Assembling nearly 300 ships from several dozen nations was an event of global cooperation. Events leading to Operation Sail 1976 commenced on May 2, in Plymouth, England, where schoolships from all over the world converged for the start of a three-stage race to Newport, Rhode Island. Led by the British schooner *Sir Winston Churchill* (on her first trans-Atlantic crossing), the fleet set sail for Tenerife in the Canary Islands. On May 23, the ships left Tenerife to complete the second leg of the race—a 2,500 mile jaunt to Hamilton Harbor in Bermuda.

The ships were scheduled to complete the final segment of the race by 7:00 P.M. June 26. They were expected to begin arriving in Newport Harbor during the two days prior to the official finish. Rhode Island residents prepared for the coming ships with a mixture of anticipation and apprehension. Some city officials lamented their fate as hosts of the greatest sailing event of the century. They feared their city would not be able to handle the expected crush of tourists. But excitement was high: berths were readied and welcoming parties planned; daily newspaper bulletins kept people posted on the progress of the vessels.

In Bermuda on the afternoon of June 20, tall and small ships jostled for a favorable starting position for the historic race. To increase maneuverability all ships were permitted to use their engines during the crowded start. When the English frigate *HMS Eskimo* fired a cannon, the race was on. With sails unfurled and engines running, the ships, according to *New York Times* reporter William Wallace, "attacked the 1.8-mile-long starting line with all the pushy vigor of dinghy sailors."

In the confusion two accidents occurred: the *Erawan* of Sweden stalled, and the Spanish ship *Juan Sebastian de Elcano* was squeezed between the *Gloria* from Colombia and the *Sagres II* from Portugal. The Argentinian ship *Libertad*, which had cut diagonally forward in an aggressive start, rammed the larger *Elcano*. The Spanish ship lost 60 feet of her 180-foot mast and was forced to leave the race, but the *Libertad* sailed away unharmed. In a lesser incident, the American museum ship *Gazela Primeiro* scraped the Romanian ship *Mircea*. The *Gazela* lost 68 feet of her mast, and was also forced to leave the race.

Although marred by two collisions, the start of the final leg of the trans-Atlantic race presented a majestic picture. The great sailing ships moved away in an 18-knot wind. But their flying start was not destined to continue: for two days the sailing ships floated motionless on a still ocean.

Cadets on the United States Coast Guard training vessel *Eagle* war-whooped a wind dance. To pass the time the Americans exchanged visits with cadets from the Russian ship *Kruzenshtern*, becalmed nearby. The Tall Ships had been similarly becalmed en route to Bermuda, and had been forced to use engine power to reach the British harbor on schedule. (Smaller ships, which were able to take advantage of lesser gusts, continued to Newport unaffected.) The British and American Sail Training Associations contacted the ships' captains and with their approval advanced the finish of the race from 7:00 P.M. June 26, to 6:00 P.M. June 24th. The *Gorch Fock* from Germany was declared the winner through a complicated series of handicapping computations; the Chilean ship *Esmeralda* finished in last place.

The Tall Ships entered Newport Harbor powered by their engines, not by canvas, for the Bicentennial would not be postponed. Again on schedule, the *Libertad*, the first of the Tall Ships to arrive, motored into Newport in the early morning of June 26. A Navy fireboat extended the traditional welcome by firing great streams of water into the air. The *Libertad* fired a 21-gun salute with her cadets "manning the yards"—standing high on the ship's superstructure. The National Guard responded with howitzer fire. All day long the tall ships continued to arrive.

In a scene that was to be reenacted at every port along the ships' journey, private boats of every description rushed to greet them. Old boats, some seeming barely able to stay afloat, ferry boats crammed with paying passengers, and tiny speedboats bustled around the giant guests. Coast Guard patrol boats, watchful and harassed, did their best to prevent collisions.

On land, enthusiastic tourists were a marked contrast to the normally reserved Newport sophisticates. As the day progressed, their numbers swelled from 95,000 to 150,000. By evening the glittering lights of the anchored ships and the exuberance of the crowds created a carnival atmosphere.

The tall and small ships spent the weekend in Newport before beginning their final trek to New York on July 1. The morning of their departure was not promising. Dense fog in the harbor lowered visibility to less than 50 feet. For a while, everything was again chaos and disorder, with officials wringing their hands in anxiety. The Tall Ships sat motionless. Periodically small ships vanished as they slipped away to sea. By midmorning the fog began to lift, and by the time the *Eagle* assumed leadership of the fleet, the sky was bright and sunny. The Tall Ships sailed under Newport Bridge, circled the bay and headed out to sea.

The Tall Ships sailed down the coast and along the south bank of Long Island, heading for anchorages in Gravesend Bay and the bight of Sandy Hook; the smaller ships made their way through Long Island Sound. The less lofty vessels anchored for the night (July 2) along the north and south shores of the Sound. Communities lucky enough to be host to some of these ships scheduled welcoming festivities and were received on board.

The Tall Ships arrived at their anchorages during the night of July 2, and entertained guests the following morning. At about midday July 3, the smaller boats gathered at Throgs Neck Bridge, proceeded down the East River through Hell Gate, and joined their taller cousins.

Meanwhile, the 53 modern warships of the International Naval Review, representing some 26 nations, began their part in the nation's birthday celebration. On July 2, a 30-mile-long column of warships assembled in the Atlantic Ocean 232 miles from New York. Three divisions of ships fell into formation behind the guided-missile cruisers *USS Wainwright* and *USS Farragut*, and the guided-missile destroyer *USS William V. Pratt*, and headed for the Hudson River.

On July 3 the warships proceeded under the Verrazano-Narrows Bridge in a 13-mile-long column. In a slow parade of military strength, British and Portuguese navy frigates, Swedish minelayers, Israeli missile boats and Canadian and Venezuelan destroyers, along with some of the most modern ships of the United States Navy, were anchored two-deep on the Brooklyn side of the river, and single-file along the opposite shore. By early afternoon the *USS Forrestal*, the enormous American aircraft carrier, was anchored off Staten Island, ready to receive some 3,000 dignitaries.

As soon as the warships arrived, pleasure boats swarmed around them. Thousands of spectators, but not as many as anticipated, lined the shores of the Hudson River. Pleasure craft endlessly circled sailing ships anchored below the Verrazano Bridge. Everything was in readiness as the day ended.

Sails of a four-masted bark (ship pictured is the **Nippon Maru**)

1. Bowsprit
2. Martingale
3. Figurehead
4. Flying jib
5. Outer jib
6. Inner jib
7. Fore topmast staysail

8. Foremast
9. Fore royal
10. Fore upper topgallant sail
11. Fore lower topgallant sail
12. Fore upper topsail
13. Fore lower topsail
14. Foresail, Fore course

15. Main royal staysail
16. Main topgallant staysail
17. Main middle staysail
18. Main topmast staysail
19. Mainmast
20. Main royal
21. Main upper topgallant sail

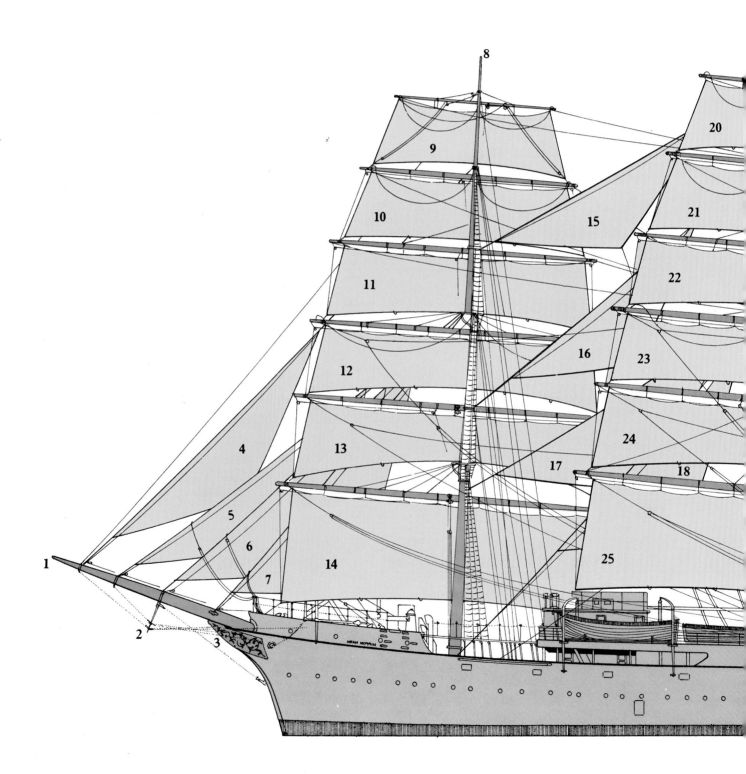

22. Main lower topgallant sail
23. Main upper topsail
24. Main lower topsail
25. Mainsail, Main course
26. Mizzen royal staysail
27. Mizzen topgallant staysail
28. Mizzen middle staysail
29. Mizzen topmast staysail
30. Mizzen mast
31. Mizzen royal
32. Mizzen upper topgallant sail
33. Mizzen lower topgallant sail
34. Mizzen upper topsail
35. Mizzen lower topsail
36. Crossjack, Mizzen course
37. Jigger topgallant staysail
38. Jigger topmast staysail
39. Jigger staysail
40. Jigger mast
41. Gaff topsail
42. Spanker

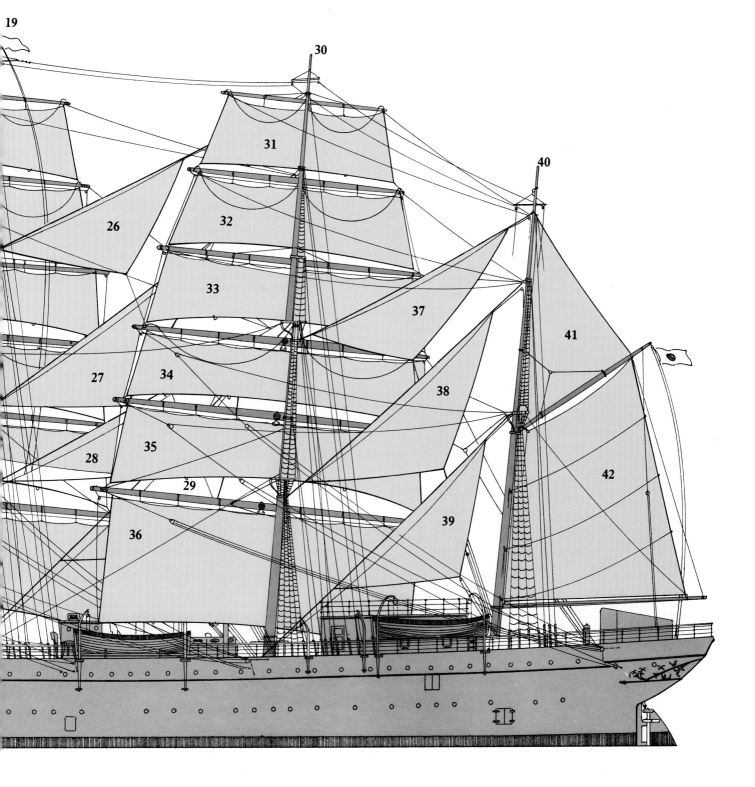

Classification of sailboats

Staysail schooner

Brigantine

Three-masted staysail schooner

Jib-headed ketch

Bark

Barkentine

Jib-headed cutter

Yawl

Brig

Full-rigged ship

The Italian naval training vessel **Amerigo Vespucci** is named for the 16th century Florentine explorer whose family name was given to the American continent. Her design gives the impression that she is a 19th century wooden frigate, but her steel construction is entirely modern. Built in 1931 at Castellamare, Italy, she is as regally outfitted as a clipper ship. Her lines are tied up with an elegant sash, and her stern is decorated with fanciful carvings.

Built in 1953, for the Spanish Navy, the barkentine **Esmeralda** is a sistership to the *Juan Sebastian de Elcano*. While still unfinished, she was purchased by the Chilean Navy for use as a schoolship. Cadets (center) learn to use muscle power on a sailing ship. Officers' quarters (upper and lower right) are beautifully finished.

The **Danmark** was built for the Danish Government in 1932, as a schoolship for the merchant marine. In 1939, she sailed to the United States for the World's Fair and remained in American waters throughout World War II. During the war she saw service as a Coast Guard training vessel. The Coast Guard was so impressed with the merits of sail training, it purchased the *Eagle* (ex-*Horst Wessel* of Nazi Germany) after the *Danmark* returned home in 1945.

The **Kruzenshtern** is one of the most magnificent sailing ships in the world. Originally named the *Padua*, she was built in Hamburg, Germany, in 1926, for the famous Laeisz Flying "P" line. As the *Padua*, the great ship worked the Chilean nitrate trade and the Australian grain trade. She was taken over by the Soviet Union in 1946, and rebuilt as a schoolship to train merchant sailors. She was renamed for a famous Russian explorer.

From 1933 to 1937, the German government had four nearly identical barks built as naval training vessels at the Blohm and Voss shipyards in Hamburg. One of these ships, the *Albert Leo Schlageter*, built in 1937, was taken by the United States at the end of the war. When she was turned over to Brazil in 1948, her name was changed to *Guanabara*. That same year she was purchased by Portugal and renamed the **Sagres II**, replacing an older training ship of that name.

The **Tovaristsch**, originally the *Gorch Fock*, was built at the Blohm and Voss yards in Hamburg in 1933. She is the sister-ship of the other pre-war German training ships, now the *Mircea*, the *Sagres II*, and the *Eagle*, as well as of the later *Gorch Fock*, a slightly enlarged version of the same design. The original *Gorch Fock* sank off Stralsund, in 1945, and was brought up by Russian salvage experts in 1948. She was refitted and in 1951 became a Soviet Navy training vessel.

The **Christian Radich** was built for the Christiania Schoolship Association in Oslo in 1939. Christian Radich had given funds to the sail training school for a deepwater ship, provided the vessel was named for him. The *Christian Radich* was taken over by the German Navy in 1940. At the end of World War II, she was discovered half-submerged with her masts and yards missing. She was raised, returned to her owners and repaired.

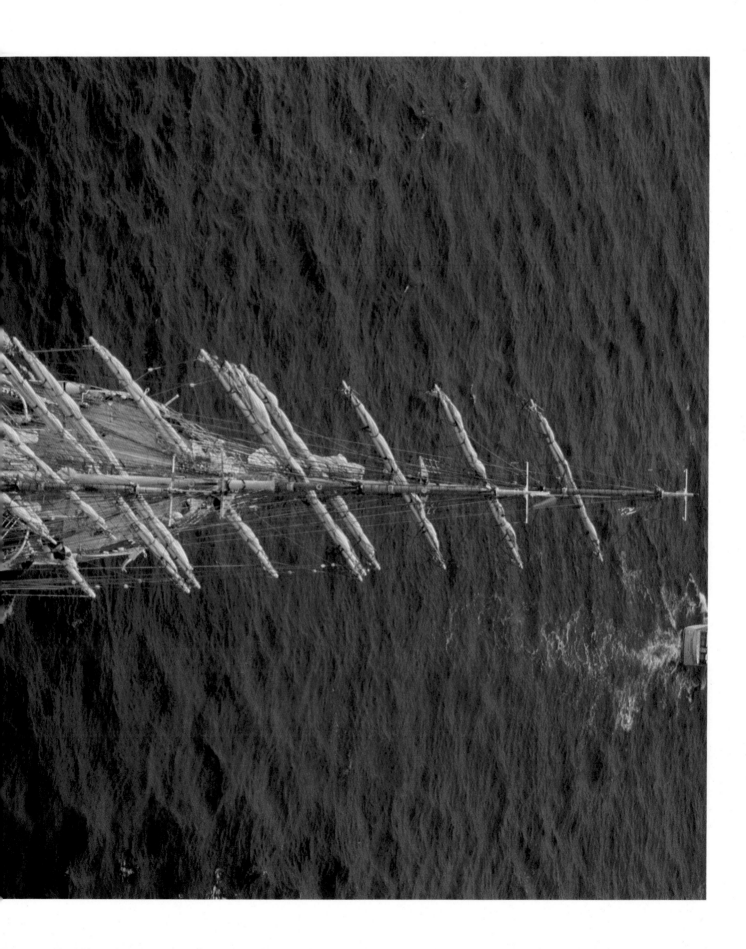

The **Juan Sebastian de Elcano** was named after the Spanish explorer who returned with the only remaining ship of Magellan's five-ship fleet in 1526. Magellan himself perished during the epic voyage, and Elcano became known as the first Spaniard to circle the globe. The Spanish topsail schooner was designed in England, and built in 1927, in Cadiz, Spain, by Echevarrieta y Larrinaga as a sail-training vessel for the Spanish Royal Navy.

The **Mircea** (below), named for a 14th century Romanian prince, was built in 1938, by the Blohm and Voss yards in Hamburg, Germany as a sail-training ship for Romania. She is one of four sisterships constructed in the 1930s.

The **Nippon Maru** (right) was built in 1930, as a training ship for officers in the Japanese merchant marine. During World War II, she was converted into an engine-powered vessel, then recommissioned as a sailing ship in 1952.

The **Dar Pomorza** was built in 1909, as a schoolship for the German merchant marine. In 1929, the people of Pomorze purchased her from a private French owner and gave her to the Polish State Sea Training School. Her name means "gift of Pomorze."

The bark **Gorch Fock** was built in 1958 in Hamburg, Germany, by Blohm and Voss as a training ship for the German Navy. She is 26 feet longer than her sisterships, the four nearly identical auxiliary barks built by Blohm and Voss between 1933 and 1937.

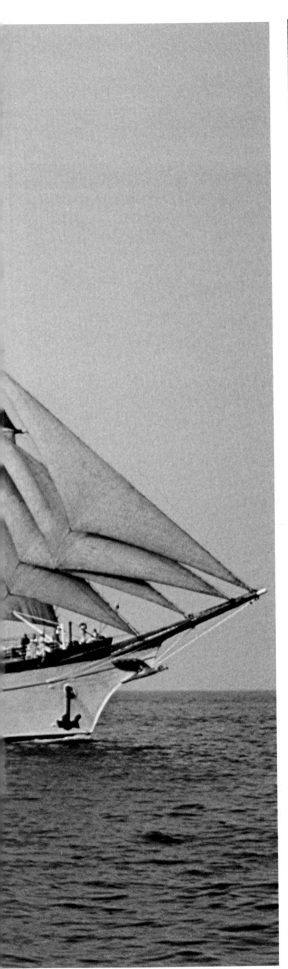

Built in 1960, at La Plata, Argentina, the full-rigged ship **Libertad** is one of the newest of the world's fleet of tall sailing ships. With a displacement of 3,765 tons, she is also one of the largest.

The bark **Gloria** is the newest tall sailing ship. She was built in 1968, at Bilbao, Spain, and is one of the largest vessels of her type in the world. She is a naval training ship run by the Armada Nacional de Colombia.

The United States Coast Guard sail-training bark **Eagle** was built in 1936, by the firm of Blohm and Voss in Hamburg, Germany. She was the second of the four sisterships produced by the Hamburg yard prior to World War II. She is a slightly larger version of the ship that preceded her, the original *Gorch Fock*, now the Russian ship *Tovaristsch*. The *Eagle* was the host ship of Operation Sail 1976.

The oldest Tall Ship taking part in Operation Sail, the **Gazela Primeiro** was built in Cocilhas, Portugal in 1883. She was made entirely from pine, and her owners, the Philadelphia Maritime Museum, boast that nearly every plank and beam in her is original. At the start of the Bermuda-to-Newport race, the *Gazela* was involved in a collision which broke her main mast. She was repaired by shipwrights in Mystic, Connecticut in time for the parade.

A ship's figurehead may represent her owner, an animal or a sea god. The figure on the **Mircea** (lower right), is the Romanian prince for whom the ship was named. Figureheads are among the oldest symbolic art in the world. In ancient times an actual sacrifice was made and the remains fastened to the bow; these bizarre decorations were replaced by wood carvings. In the 17th century figureheads and stern carvings became wildly ornate.

The **Gladan** is a 129-foot fore-and-aft schooner. She was built in Stockholm in 1947, as a training ship for the Swedish Royal Navy. Sweden boasts a substantial fleet of sailing ships, including several large vessels operated as floating museums.

The schooner **Zawisza Czarny**, built in 1952 as a fishing trawler, is now a training ship owned by the Polish Pathfinders' Union of Gdynia. There are several sailing clubs in Poland and quite a fleet of sailing ships, including the *Dar Pomorza*.

Unlike most of the ships in the Operation Sail parade, the **Barba Negra** was a working commercial sailing ship until 1956. Built in Norway in 1896, she is a classic Baltic schooner and was active in European fishing, whaling, and trading until her retirement. Her current owner, Albert Siedl, purchased her in 1970, and rerigged her as a barkentine for the West Indies charter trade. (A barkentine, like a topsail schooner, is square rigged on the foremost mast.)

The **America** is a replica of the famous schooner yacht built in 1851, the first racing yacht from the United States to win the America's Cup. The modern-day *America* was built in 1967, for the F&M Schaefer Brewing Company. With the exception of the cabin at the stern, she faithfully duplicates her predecessor in every detail.

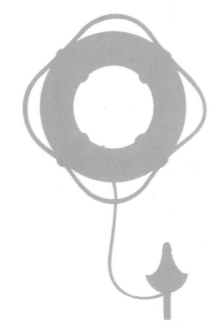

The three-masted schooner **Sir Winston Churchill** was built in Hull, England, in 1966, for the English Sail Training Association. She is gaff-rigged on her two forward masts, with a marconi-rigged mizzen. The *Sir Winston Churchill* was host ship at the outset of the race to Newport, Rhode Island, which began on May 2, 1976, at Plymouth, England. The schooner's trip to New York Harbor was her first trans-Atlantic voyage. In Bermuda, a crew of 42 young women joined her.

The barkentine **Regina Maris** belongs to the Ocean Research and Education Society of Boston. She is used as a sail-training ship and for oceanographic purposes. Using sailing ships for oceanographic research is one practical way of maintaining their numbers on the world's seas.

The three-masted schooner **Bel Espoir II** is 125 feet long and gaff-rigged. She is owned by Père Jacquen of Paris and represented France in the 1976 Operation Sail parade. Most privately-owned ships took a few trainees on board for the occasion.

The schooner **Eendracht** was built in 1974, for the Netherlands Sail Training Association. She has a gaff-rigged foremast, with a marconi-rigged main. The small Dutch fleet sent to Operation Sail delighted onlookers by sailing in formation.

Resplendent in dress uniforms, crew members of the warships anchored in New York Harbor stood in formation to salute the passing sailing ships during the Operation Sail parade.

(Left) The aircraft carrier *USS Forrestal* hosted dignitaries from all over the world during the International Naval Review, which occurred simultaneously with Operation Sail. The review concluded when the *USS Wainwright*, at the head of the column near the George Washington Bridge, moved through the anchored warships to the *Forrestal*, which was anchored near the Verrazano Bridge. Secretary of State Kissinger and Vice-President Rockefeller were the senior officials on board the *Wainwright* during the proceedings.

(Right, top) Admiral Thomas Moorer, President Gerald Ford and Secretary of the Navy J. William Middendorf II move to their bleacher seats on the flight deck of the Navy's host ship, the aircraft carrier *U.S.S. Forrestal*.

(Right, bottom) As part of the ceremonies on board the *Forrestal*, President Ford rang the ship's bell 13 times in honor of the 13 original colonies.

A Portuguese warship moves into position on the Hudson River. An armada of naval vessels from 26 nations arrived in New York Harbor on July 3 to participate in the International Naval Review on the following day. They remained at anchor in the Hudson during July 4, and then moved to berths at the city's piers. During the next three days, the warships welcomed thousands of interested persons aboard.

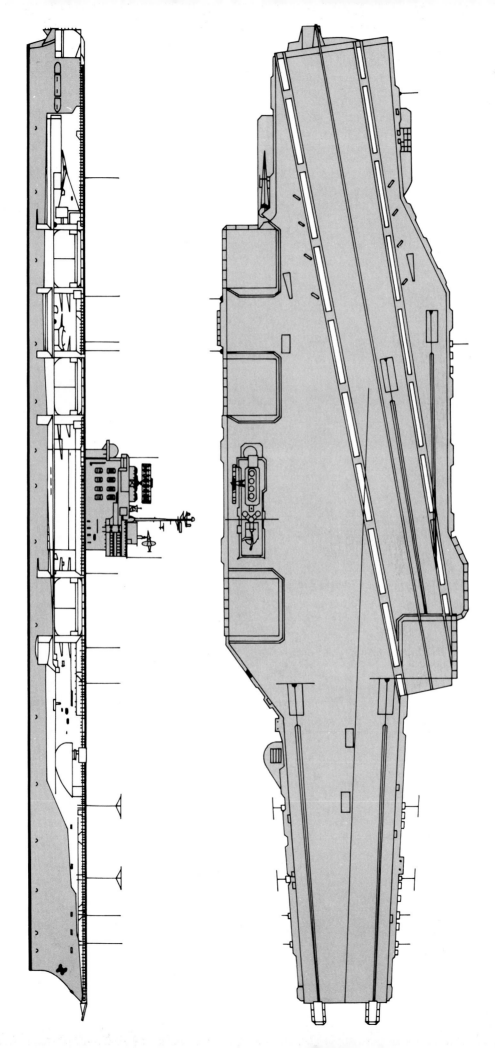

The Forrestal was the world's first aircraft carrier designed and built after World War II. Advances in aviation influenced the design of aircraft carriers, and the Forrestal was the first aircraft carrier built specifically to handle jet-propelled aircraft. Some improvements include angled flight deck, steam catapults and internal compartmentation to reduce effects of conventional and nuclear attack.

Operation Sail
July 4, 1976: The Hudson River

When the sun's first light struck the nation on July 4, 1976 (at 4:31 A.M. at Mars Hill, Maine), Operation Sail was ready. After months of preparation, scores of paid and volunteer workers held their breaths and hoped for sunshine. City officials feared mass confusion (some had predicted "another Woodstock") and prayed for a holiday without incident. Thousands of New York residents scurried to West Side apartments or piers for a clear view of the water. Others left the city for the hinterlands and a clear view of a television screen.

Without a doubt Operation Sail 1976 was one of the sailing events of the century. It was highly publicized in connection with the American Bicentennial, but the concept of the event is at least 20 years old. In 1956, the Sail Training Association of England hosted the first international gathering of sailing ships at Dartmouth, England. It was so successful that sailing ships gathered again in France in 1958, in Norway in 1960, and in Belgium in 1962.

The first Operation Sail, in 1964, was the brainstorm of New York artist and sailing enthusiast Nils Hansell. He proposed the idea of a trans-Atlantic sailing ship race to Commodore John S. Baylis, a former Captain of the Port of New York. With the help of Baylis and Frank Braynard of the American Merchant Marine Institute, Hansell secured the cooperation of the United States government.

Braynard and Hansell contacted foreign ministries to request the participation of their schoolships. Then they asked the Sail Training Association of England to sponsor the start of a trans-Atlantic race that would bring the ships into New York Harbor during the 1964 World's Fair. The 25 vessels that eventually sailed into New York Harbor included 11 of the world's biggest schoolships. Similar Operation Sail events were repeated during the late 1960s and early 1970s, but the 1976 fleet is by far the largest. It also boasts the greatest international participation thus far.

Frank Braynard was the man behind the 1976 Operation Sail. Immediately after Operation Sail 1964 was finished, Braynard began considering a repeat performance. In 1972, Braynard asked the English Sail Training Association to synchronize their biennial sailing event with the American Bicentennial. The English agreed, and Braynard began to make preparations. In 1974, the New York Port Authority donated office space at the World Trade Center, and the states of New York and New Jersey donated Bicentennial funds.

A similar precedent had been set for the International Naval Review which comprised the second part of the water spectacle. In 1893, the First International Naval Review was held also in New York Harbor to commemorate the 400th anniversary of the discovery of America by Christopher Columbus. In 1907 a second review was held at Hampton Roads, Virginia, in honor of the 300th anniversary of the founding of Jamestown, Virginia, the first settlement in the United States. The Third International Naval Review was also held at Hampton Roads, in 1957, in honor of Jamestown's 350th anniversary. But the 1976 Fourth International Naval Review, held in conjunction with Operation Sail, was the largest event of its kind: 53 ships from 26 nations attended.

The morning of the Fourth of July was bright and cool in New York City. It was not perfect weather—the sky was overcast and the day remained hazy but bright—but public enthusiasm and participation made up for the lack of sunshine. The harbor was as crowded as a highway on a holiday weekend: 30,000 pleasure craft (including a rubber raft propelled by an outboard motor), all dwarfed by the cruisers and sailing ships, hurried through the congested waters. Spectators on land were also infected with the sailing ship fever. Manhattan merchants experienced what one clerk called a "binocular riot." West Side apartment residents suddenly found themselves with dozens of close friends who wanted to view the parade from their rooftops or living rooms, and suburanites were searching out long-lost Manhattan relatives. Out-of-state tourists set up camp in the parks. Some 6 million people from the shores of New York City alone (not counting New Jersey spectators) watched Operation Sail and the International Naval Review.

People perched in trees and climbed cranes and tractors. They wormed their way through barricades to watch from prohibited areas. Old people sat in chairs under umbrellas, babies and children zipped about them. The city's various boat lines, such as the Staten Island ferry, and the Circle Line ships, offered a closer look. Both required reservations. The wealthy sailed their own yachts into designated spectator areas or rented boats for the day.

Bicentennial organizers as well as commercial enterprises provided special viewing areas. Seventeen thousand bleacher seats were set up near Battery Park. Brokerage offices in the Wall Street area were opened on Sunday. The landlord of the World Trade Center carefully parceled out space at the rate of 120 square feet per person. It was possible to rent helicopters, usually servicing La Guardia and Newark airports, for a half-hour bird's-eye view of the spectacle. Restaurants overlooking the harbor offered lunch — and a comfortable viewing spot.

The anchored naval vessels also provided seating for privileged guests. The aircraft-carrier *USS Forrestal* hosted 3,000 visiting dignitaries. President Ford was among them, briefly. He arrived by helicopter, but was off again to officiate elsewhere in the nation.

The only serious miscalculation concerned an enormous American flag designed to hang on the Verrazano-Narrows Bridge, marking the start of the parade route. The nylon taffeta creation had the dimensions of a football field-and-a-half and was to hang 250 feet above the water. But the oversized flag was blown to shreds some days before the Fourth.

Even without the flag, the *Eagle* passed under the Verrazano Bridge on schedule at pre-

cisely 11:00 A.M. The crew members were aloft in the ship's rigging and spread out along the yardarms. In stately procession behind the *Eagle* came 15 Tall Ships from 14 nations and the accompanying flotilla of smaller craft.

As each ship passed the *Forrestal*, anchored just above the bridge, the crew manned the yards and saluted the carrier. Sailors cheered and waved. Crews on the stationary warships stood at the rail in colorful dress uniforms and saluted each sailing vessel in her turn.

At 12 o'clock all the warships in the harbor fired a simultaneous 21-gun salute. By 1:30 in the afternoon, the *Eagle* had passed under the George Washington Bridge. Originally she was to continue to Spuyten Duyvil, but she turned about to retrace her path downriver.

At about the same time, the cruiser *USS Wainwright*, with Vice-President Rockefeller and Secretary of State Kissinger on board, made her slow, careful way through the crowded river to the *Forrestal*. As the *Wainwright* reached the *Forrestal*, the International Naval Review concluded. Operation Sail 1976 concluded at about 5:00 P.M.

As *New York Times* reporter McCandlish Phillips remarked, most of the spectators who thronged the shores throughout the day couldn't "tell a schooner from a lobster bisque." But they read their programs faithfully and tried valiantly to distinguish a topsail schooner from a barkentine. One enterprising onlooker brought his own loudspeaker and announced the name of each craft as it sailed by. His friends and fellow spectators cheered each passing vessel.

Enthusiasm far outweighed any lack of expertise. Spectator excitement was undampened even by two unexpected late-afternoon rain squalls. Viewers took the drenching with aplomb. Many refused to relinquish desirable vantage points. On the whole the crowds displayed remarkably good spirits that reigned throughout the day.

LIBRARY
MEDWAY HIGH SCHOOL

(Preceding page) The *Gorch Fock* (far right), the *Libertad* (center right), the *Kruzenshtern* (center left), and the *Dar Pomorza* (far left) begin to sail away at the glorious start of the race from Bermuda to Newport, R.I. The Bermuda-to-Newport race was the third leg of a three-part trans-Atlantic race for many of the same sailing ships which took part in Operation Sail 1976. The historic race began on May 2, in Plymouth, England. First the ships raced to Tenerife in the Canary Islands, then to Bermuda, and finally they set sail for Newport on June 20.

(Left) Sailors make sail on the *Danmark*. The Danish school-ship is government-owned and normally carries 80 sail-training cadets in addition to her crew.

(Right) Japanese sailors aboard the *Nippon Maru* salute another vessel by waving their caps and manning the bowsprit.

Becalmed enroute to Newport during the Bermuda-to-Newport leg of the three-stage trans-Atlantic race, the United States Coast Guard bark *Eagle* barely drifts on a motionless sea. For two days the Tall Ships lay trapped upon the calm waters. Finally, race officials decided to move the finish forward and asked ships' captains to motor to Newport after the official end of the race.

(Left) Hundreds of lines organize the complicated rigging of the *Amerigo Vespucci*. In earlier times sailing ships often had a "donkey engine"—a steam engine with a drum to which all the major lines ran—to assist in hoisting sails. While much of the work can still be done by hand, all of the modern ships have mechanical devices for back-up.

(Right) Members of the crew of the *Libertad* make everything shipshape before the start of the Bermuda-to-Newport race. Shortly after the race began, the *Libertad* was involved in an accident that left the *Juan Sebastian de Elcano* with 60 feet of her 180-foot main mast missing.

(Following page) Lights on the sailing ships turn Newport Harbor into the glittering midway of a carnival. Tall and small ships spent the better part of a week at Newport, before embarking on July 2 for New York and Operation Sail.

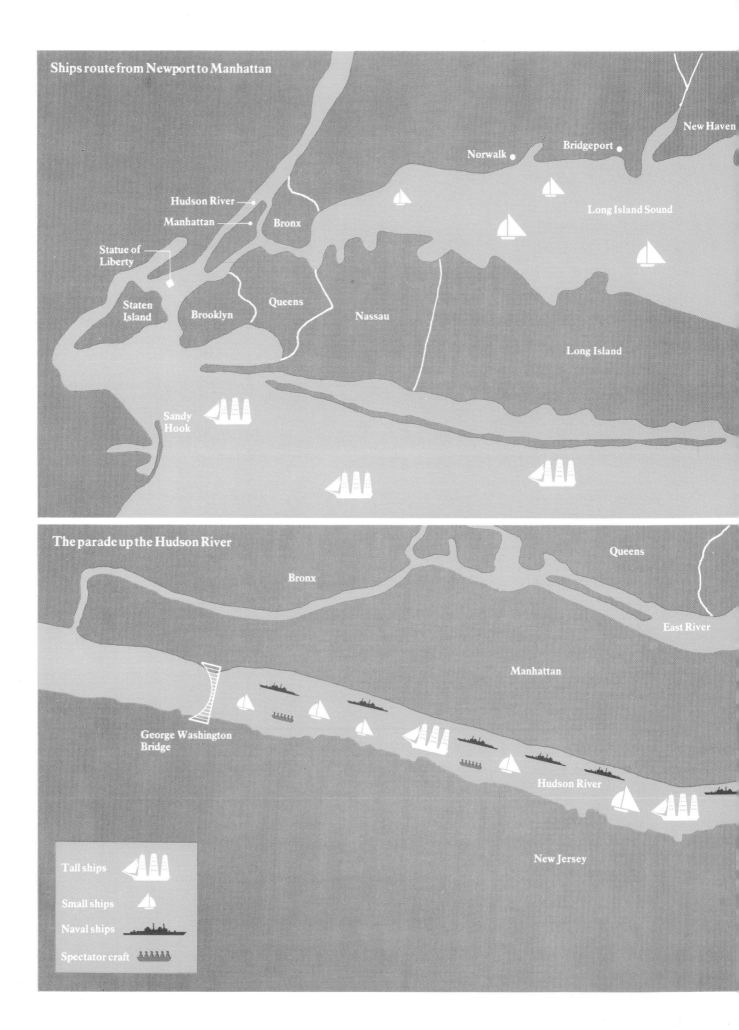

Ships route from Newport to Manhattan

New Haven

Norwalk

Bridgeport

Long Island Sound

Hudson River

Manhattan

Bronx

Statue of
Liberty

Staten
Island

Brooklyn

Queens

Nassau

Long Island

Sandy
Hook

The parade up the Hudson River

Queens

Bronx

East River

Manhattan

George Washington
Bridge

Hudson River

New Jersey

Tall ships

Small ships

Naval ships

Spectator craft

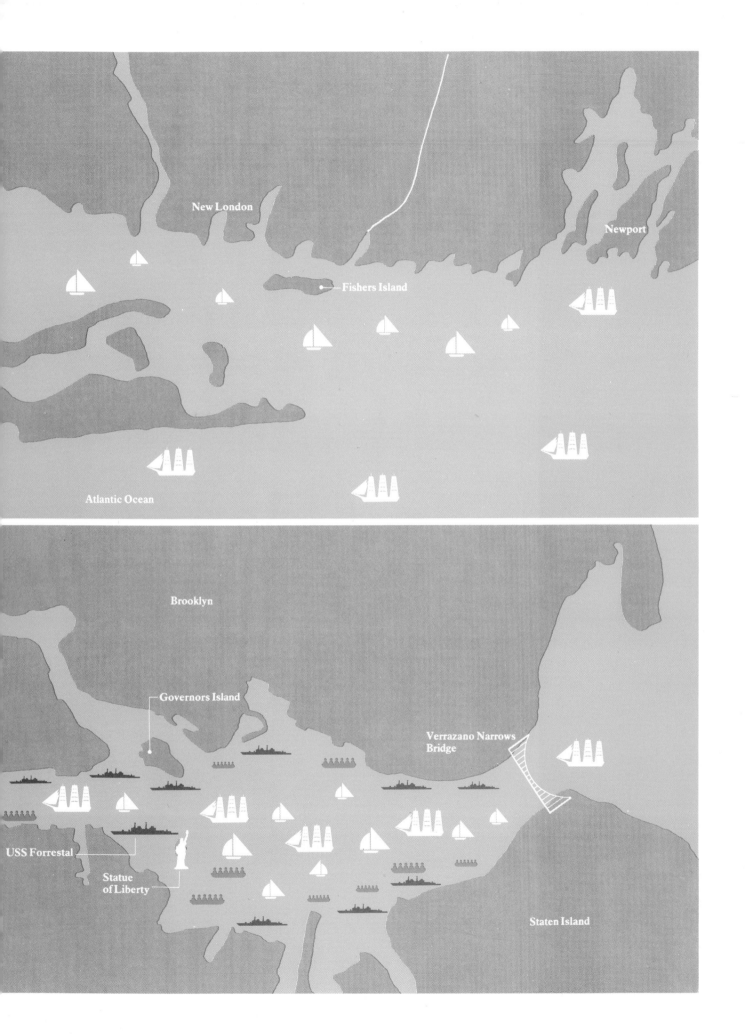

New London

Newport

Fishers Island

Atlantic Ocean

Brooklyn

Governors Island

Verrazano Narrows
Bridge

USS Forrestal

Statue
of Liberty

Staten Island

At precisely 11:00 A.M. July 4, 1976, the Operation Sail parade began. As host ship, the United States Coast Guard training ship *Eagle* led the way under the Verrazano Bridge and up the Hudson River. Behind her sailed the 15 Tall Ships from 14 nations, hundreds of smaller sail-training vessels and a multitude of pleasure craft of all descriptions.

(Preceding page) New York Harbor resembled the nation's highways on the Fourth of July. The sea was unpredictable as usual, and the weather underwent drastic changes as the day progressed. Sudden rain squalls in the late afternoon effectively drenched participants and spectators alike, and brought the parade to a somewhat premature conclusion.

(Left) Aboard the *Nippon Maru* sailors lash the furled sails to the yardarms. Though routine, it's quite a job: the big Japanese sail-training ship has 25,800 square feet of sail area.

(Right) Crew members of the *Danmark* splice line. Since steel ships took over the shipbuilding industry around the turn of the century, ships' rigging has been made from steel cable.

(Preceding page) This aerial view of the deck of the *Libertad* indicates the height of her masts. Those who believe in training under sail say that the measure of a man is known when he is working 150 feet in the air and standing on nothing but rope. His character is further tested under the stress of heavy winds or storm conditions. "One hand for the ship, one for yourself."

(Left) The ship's bell is used as a signalling device and also to tell time. To mark time, it is rung every half-hour in four-hour watches. Beginning at 12:30, the bell is rung once, then twice at 1:00, and so on until "eight bells" are rung at 4:00. The cycle is then repeated.

(Right) The tall mast of a full-rigged ship. The term "full-rigged" indicates that a ship has square sails on all of her masts. Wind pressure on the towering structures can be tremendous; it was not so unusual for a ship to be dismasted entirely during a passage around Cape Horn.

The Hudson River had probably never seen so many craft at once. The Coast Guard feared it would not be able to keep order. But few mishaps occurred and accidents were minor. The gigantic aircraft carrier *USS Forrestal* (lower left), the largest carrier ever built, dwarfs every other ship in sight.

(Following page) With flags flying across her masts from bow to stern, the Russian ship *Kruzenshtern* has "dressed ship." As she passes the *USS Forrestal*, her crew also "mans the yards"—stands along the ship's yardarms—in perfect symmetry. The crew on the warship returns the gesture with a salute. The *Kruzenshtern*, originally the *Padua* of the Laeisz Flying "P" line, was the last cargo-carrying, four-masted bark ever built.

(Left, top) Dutch sailors man the yards and wave enthusiastically. A small fleet of sailing ships arrived from Holland for Operation Sail.

(Left, bottom) People stood in line for hours to ride the Staten Island ferry on the Fourth of July. Others bought seats in advance on Day Line cruise ships.

(Above) Those who owned boats were likely to suddenly find themselves very popular during the week of the festivities. In Newport, R.I., a little ferry boat greets the arriving sailing ships.

Surrounded by a bevy of schooners, cabin cruisers and large and small speed boats, the United States Coast Guard bark *Eagle* makes her way up the Hudson River. In addition to the 300 ships officially taking part in Operation Sail and the International Naval Review, thousands of pleasure craft choked New York Harbor. Fortunately, accidents were negligible.

(Left) The South African warship *President Kruger* is anchored in front of the Statue of Liberty. Her crew stands at attention to salute the passing sailing ships.

(Above) Crew members on board the Tall Ships return the salute of the sailors aboard the naval vessels. Sailors on the Italian ship *Amerigo Vespucci* stand at attention in pyramidal columns on the ratlines.

(Left, top and bottom) Almost everything went exactly as planned on the Fourth of July. One of the few exceptions was the football-field-and-a-half-sized flag made for the Verrazano Bridge – the start of the parade route. It blew down almost immediately.

(Right, top) Tall and small ships turned and headed back down the Hudson after reaching the George Washington Bridge. They were originally to have continued to Spuyten Duyvil. Spectators further upstream complained vociferously.

(Right, bottom) So many sailing ships in one place can lead to a more disastrous result. Off Bermuda, just two weeks before Operation Sail, there were three separate collisions involving four of the Tall Ships.

(Left) Extending her traditional salute, a little fireboat spouts great streams of water from several hoses at once.

(Right) In Fort Lee, New Jersey, apartment dwellers watch the Operation Sail parade from their balconies.

(Following page) Public officials maintained that Fourth of July crowds in New York City were much lighter than anticipated, but the situation at the foot of the World Trade Center makes it seem hardly possible. The giant towers offered some of the best views of Operation Sail in the city.

(Left, top) Spectators jam roofs on Manhattan's West Side to glimpse the passing ships in the Operation Sail parade.

(Left, bottom) Hundreds of thousands of people poured into New York City to board the docked ships. Pier 86 on the Hudson River is water-to-water

people. *Esmeralda*, *Gloria*, *Nippon Maru*, *Libertad*, and a dozen smaller training ships were all docked there.

(Right) The *Esmeralda* is framed by buildings, stoplights and crowds as she passes near the shore during Operation Sail.

(Left) Cadets from the *Great Britain II* drink champagne in Newport, R.I. The 85-foot-long ketch is famous as an around-the-world racing yacht.

(Right) The all-woman cadet crew of the *Sir Winston Churchill* made her unique among the sail-training ships taking part in Operation Sail. In Newport, the *Churchill*'s cadets, egged on by cadets from the *Great Britain II*, fight to win a tug-of-war.

(Following page) Warships at each of the Hudson River piers had a string of colorful signal flags flying – the traditional decoration in honor of a special occasion. Officials and a few privileged persons awaited the arrival of tall and small sailing ships after the Operation Sail parade.

After the conclusion of Operation Sail, three of the ships—*Gloria*, *Nippon Maru* and *Esmeralda*—docked at Pier 86 on the Hudson River. On July 5th close to a million people boarded and inspected these and other tall ships as well as 49 vessels of the International Naval Review.

The Celebration
Music, festivals and fairs

For the army of people who helped organize the nation-wide Bicentennial celebrations, as well as for the millions who enjoyed the fruits of those labors, it seemed hardly possible that July 4, 1976, had finally arrived.

For a while it had seemed the Bicentennial might fizzle. In 1975, some wondered if the United States had anything to celebrate. Then all of a sudden there it was. And the people, although bombarded by commercialism, scolded by those who scorned it, and inundated with debate about the appropriateness of the celebration, went out and had a good time.

Traditionally, the Fourth of July is a low-key holiday; a leisurely day of family fun, maybe a few fireworks at home, a picnic and then, in the evening, a visit to the local fireworks display with an ice cream on the way home. Many citizens were relieved to discover that for the most part, the nation would celebrate the Bicentennial in the traditional way. Parades, church suppers and red-white-and-blue bandstands were still the order of the day.

For example, in Bartow, Florida, the townspeople held their customary celebration to honor the birthday (134th) of Charlie Smith. Mr. Smith is not sure of his age, but the Social Security Administration acknowledges him to be the oldest living American. He was brought to the United States in 1854 on a slave ship.

In Washington, D.C. President Ford dedicated the new Air and Space Museum of the Smithsonian Institute. In the evening there was a Fourth of July parade and a fireworks display. But the Capitol's fireworks were among the most impressive in the nation. Instead of the normal two tons of explosives, nearly 33½ tons illuminated the night sky. Philadelphia, home of the Continental Congress and the Declaration of Independence, hosted the longest Fourth of July parade in its history—the event lasted five hours. The Los Angeles County Bicentennial parade was advertised as the longest in the nation. This one stretched almost eleven miles.

Perhaps the most rigorous demonstration of patriotism took place in Alaska. Nearly 1,000 hardy souls climbed to the top of Mount McKinley, the highest peak in North America. Possibly the most meaningful demonstration took place in Chicago: the Immigration and Naturalization Service swore in 1,776 brand new citizens in the Chicago stadium. But the eyes of the nation focused on the celebration in New York City, "Salute '76." The arrival of the Tall Ships and their fellows from nations all around the world generated national interest. As the ships sailed up the Hudson, Manhattan Island sprouted a colorful collection of land fairs.

The land events focused on a single theme: "July Fourth in Old New York." Some 50 open-air events squeezed into the southern, and oldest, section of the city, from the Battery to City Hall. Pavillions, some several blocks long, represented 22 different ethnic cultures. The Fulton Fish Market presented its own festival, and the South Street Seaport Museum provided additional entertainment.

July 3 was a preview of events to follow. While some people watched the ships maneuvering into the harbor, twenty ethnic groups presented native songs and dances at the Heritage Festival at Rockefeller Center. The same evening New York held its first after-dark parade. Nichiren Shoshu Academy, an international organization for the promotion of world peace, sponsored floats which traveled up 6th Avenue to Central Park. In the harbor's evening darkness the Statue of Liberty could be seen decked out in special lights for the occasion.

The celebration of the Fourth of July commenced with an 8:00 A.M. ecumenical service in Battery Park. Mayor Beame's civic ceremonies began at nine o'clock. One of the events included a reading of the Declaration of Independence by conductor-composer Leonard Bernstein. Shortly before the conclusion of the ceremonies, the Veterans Corps of Artillery discharged two cannon and fired a 50-gun salute to the Union. Gunfire was very much a part of the day's Bicentennial activities, as ships and groups on land saluted one another.

The only events that could match the repetition of the 21-gun salutes were the reading of the Declaration of Independence and the re-enactment of General George Washington's farewell address to his troops in front of Fraunces Tavern in lower Manhattan. "Washington" spoke throughout the day and every half hour someone reread the historic document at City Hall. Listeners were asked to sign a facsimile to reaffirm the egalitarian spirit of the new republic.

Red, white and blue was everywhere. FTD florists marked historical locations with tricolored blooms. The fountains in Columbus Circle and Park Avenue also featured red, white and blue decorations. Elsewhere the life and times of revolutionary days were remembered. Museums presented historical reviews, colonial craft fairs, and displays of revolutionary clothing and implements.

The popularity of the ethnic fairs was an interesting and appropriate side-effect of the Bicentennial proceedings. In examining the country's beginnings, at least some of the population has become aware of the multinational roots of the United States, and, as a result, many ethnic groups have become reacquainted with their own heritages. Fairs springing up in the city streets have long been a part of the summer scene, but the Fourth of July gave them special significance.

In keeping with the historical theme, many restaurants concentrated on colonial-style fare and modern-day patriots witnessed a symbolic beheading of George III. But it was possible to eat conch and dance the limbo at the Haitian fair or watch the Turkish belly dancers while munching spinach-and-cheese pie. Chinese-Americans performed a dragon dance, Japan-ese-Americans featured demonstrations of flower-arranging and at the Indian Pavillion spectators were shown how to drape a sari.

The Children's Plaza, which featured flag-making classes, jugglers, clowns and magic shows, ranked high in popularity. Walking tours of historic lower Manhattan were another interesting diversion.

Music was very much a part of the events of the day. There was folk dancing in the streets, and music from Irish pipers, Swedish fiddlers and Neapolitan street singers. The Newport Jazz Festival, an annual summer event since 1953, is traditionally scheduled for the July 4 holiday. In 1973, the outdoor festival relocated in New York City. In 1976, it was an added bonus to the Bicentennial activities. There were outdoor gospel concerts, and evenings of jazz at Carnegie Hall and Radio City Music Hall. On July 3, the Staten Island ferry carried some lucky individuals past the Tall Ships while dixieland bands played in the background. On the afternoon of the Fourth, Count Basie re-joined his orchestra for the first time in many years, and performed an outdoor concert at the World Trade Center.

Of course, the music of military bands and drum and bugle corps filtered through the city. At 1 New York Plaza the program featured American music of all kinds. Performers, most of whom played without charge or at a fraction of their normal rates, sang sea chanteys and gospel tunes, and played bluegrass, jazz, and country and western melodies.

At noon all the naval ships in the harbor fired a simultaneous 21-gun salute. At 2:00 o'clock church bells rang throughout lower Manhattan and all activity was momentarily suspended to commemorate the signing of the Declaration of Independence on July 4, 1776.

In the late afternoon a parade made its way from City Hall through the area of the Old New York festival. Manou Majlessi, portraying General Washington, became something of an event himself. He graciously signed dollar bills for just about anyone as he rode astride his white charger, Turtledove.

(Left, top) On July 3, New York City began Bicentennial celebrations that were to last nearly a week with its first after-dark parade. The Nichiren Shoshu Academy sponsored a parade up the Avenue of the Americas to Central Park. An 85-foot-high float of a square-rigged ship commemorated the Boston Tea Party.

(Left, bottom) The "July 4th in Old New York" festival began with an ecumenical service followed by Mayor Beame's civic ceremonies. Mayor Beame gave an address, and Leonard Bernstein read the Declaration of Independence. At the conclusion of the ceremony, the Veterans Corps of Artillery gave their traditional cannon salute to the Union.

(Right) A traditional ticker-tape parade up Broadway from Battery Park to City Hall was held for visiting crew members as part of New York City's official welcoming ceremonies. Afterward, sailors who had been enjoying their leave in a new port since July, dispersed to join the continuing celebration. The next day most of the ships departed.

(Left) "July 4th in Old New York" included readings of the words of famous Americans in front of Federal Hall on Wall Street. The present Federal Hall, completed in 1847, stands on the site of the original structure. The original Federal Hall served as the nation's first Capitol building. George Washington was inaugurated as the first President of the United States on its balcony.

(Right) At the Ukranian Festival, the Oprysko Dancers of Astoria and the Verkhovynsti Dancers of New York presented traditional folk dances. Ukranian folk songs, music and operatic arias were featured, as well as exhibitions of Ukranian arts and crafts and samples of such delicacies as borsch, holubtsi, varenyky, nalysnyky, and pyrizhky.

Late in the afternoon of July 4, a Bicentennial parade made its way from City Hall south to Battery Park. The entourage included actors costumed as Revolutionary War figures, marching bands and representatives from the various ethnic festivals.

(Top) The Philippine float featured dancing by the Philippine Dance Company of New York.

(Bottom) The Ukranian float carried musicians from the Ukranian Bandura Ensemble of New York.

(Top) Miss Norway graced the front of her country's float, while musicians played enthusiastically in the rear.

(Bottom) The West Indian float provided a mobile concert of steel-band music.

Dancing by the H.A.N.A.C.
Dance Troupe was part of the
Greek Festival. The Trojans
Band played the music while
spectators gorged on souvlaki,
shishkebab and Greek pastries.

Epilogue

By 5:00 P.M. on the afternoon of July 4th, most of the Tall Ships were berthed. Twelve were docked at Hudson River piers, numbers 84 to 92, stretching from 43rd to 52nd Streets. The other four were docked at the pier of the South Street Seaport Museum.

Evening ceremonies began with a 6:00 P.M. Evensong service at St. Paul's Chapel. St. Paul's, which dates from 1776, is the oldest church building extant in Manhattan. In 1789, George Washington and John Quincy Adams, the first President and Vice-President of the United States, worshipped at this church after being inaugurated in New York City, the nation's first capital.

At 7:30 P.M. the American Symphony Orchestra, conducted by Morton Gould, presented a concert at Battery Park. As part of the day's concluding ceremonies, New York City's Mayor Beame was presented with facsimiles of the Declaration of Independence signed by the thousands who visited City Hall.

Leonard Bernstein and the New York Philharmonic Orchestra began a concert of American music in Central Park's Sheep Meadow at 8:30 P.M. Mr. Bernstein and the Philharmonic had just completed a unique European tour. For the first time, an American orchestra presented European audiences with a program consisting wholly of works by American composers. The evening concert on the Fourth of July was the culmination of a six week, 28-concert tour. Mr. Bernstein not only conducted the orchestra, he appeared as piano soloist in George Gershwin's "Rhapsody in Blue." In keeping with Mr. Bernstein's commitment to bring fine music to the people, the concert was free.

At 9:00 P.M. those who had not given up and gone home after the long day's activities could watch one of the most spectacular displays of fireworks ever presented. Macy's department store provided the fireworks, and Walt Disney Productions choreographed the show. The fireworks were synchronized with a simultaneous radio broadcast of music and commentary, and spectators were urged to bring their portable radios with them.

The display centered around the Statue of Liberty. Theoretically, the Fourth of July is the statue's anniversary. She was supposed to be ready for the 1876 Centennial celebration, but was not finished in time. For the Bicentennial display of fireworks, 13 searchlights, positioned at the base of the statue, were turned upward to illuminate the figure. Liberty's crown glowed with special blue and green lights, and her torch burned bright gold.

The fireworks display officially began with a 200-gun salute from warships still anchored in New York Harbor. During the next half hour some 3,000 shells of fireworks were set off from six sites: Ellis Island, Liberty Island, Governor's Island and three nearby barges.

The radio broadcast was made up of patriotic music such as marches of John Philip Sousa and "America the Beautiful," and quotations from famous Americans like Rev. Dr. Martin Luther King, Jr., John F. Kennedy, George Washington, and Abraham Lincoln. Meanwhile, fireworks pulsed in time with the music. Chrysanthemums blossomed high in the air, and pinpoints of light appeared with each exploding firecracker. At times, the entire night sky became a sheet of splintering silver or gold.

A dense crowd blanketed the entire tip of Manhattan. The people yelled and applauded each flare. At the conclusion of the grand pyrotechnics, the crowd turned toward the Statue of Liberty and sang the "Star-Spangled Banner." Above the harbor, a helicopter towed a 60-by-100-foot flag composed of red, white and blue lights. After a moment of silence, church bells again rang throughout lower Manhattan.

The crowd dispersed slowly, and moved northward in a steady stream. The people were quiet and orderly as they walked in the city streets. For one day the giant metropolis had been converted to a small town. A feeling of satisfaction and comfortable exhaustion lingered, for all had gone well. Predictions of chaos and misfortune had proven unfounded.

And on July 5, the spirit of the previous day remained. Thousands of people streamed into the city to visit the Tall Ships, which were not scheduled to depart until July 7. Crowds and traffic had been lighter on the Fourth than anticipated, so congestion on July 5 came as something of a surprise. Lower Manhattan, in the area of the Fulton Fish Market and the South Street Seaport Museum, was so crowded pedestrians could barely squeeze by one another. Lines of people waiting to see the ships were stretched for over a quarter of a mile. At one point so many people crowded onto the South Street Museum pier, officials temporarily closed it. But despite the crowding and jostling, visitors on board the ships were respectful and well-mannered.

A carnival atmosphere prevailed throughout the city. Sailors wandered everywhere, and were as happy-go-lucky as the sailors in a Frank Sinatra-Gene Kelly movie. Cadets of various nationalities visited each others' ships. Young sailors on leave in a new port sought out inexpensive saloons and young women. Captain Kjell Thorsen of the Norwegian ship *Christian Radich* chose the day for his wedding. Margrethe Asslid, his bride-to-be, flew in from Oslo for the ceremony. As spectators beside the ship cheered, Captain and Mrs. Thorsen walked beneath an arch of crossed oars.

People wandered everywhere. The parks were filled with picnickers and sunbathers. Visitors meandered through the city streets, soaking up the unfamiliar atmosphere. All afternoon the "52nd Street Jazz Fair" enlivened Broadway from 50th to 54th Streets as the Newport Jazz Festival continued.

July 6 arrived and the city returned to work, but the celebration continued. The Tall Ships were still welcoming visitors, and thousands came for a look. In the afternoon, the Operation Sail/International Naval Review Land Parade was held. Groups representing all of the nations in the great maritime event marched up Broadway from Battery Park to City Hall. This is the traditional route of ticker-tape parades, and cadets and crew members were dutifully showered with confetti. At City Hall Mayor Beame officially welcomed the foreign visitors to the city.

After the welcoming address, the city treated everybody to lunch. Cadets munched giant hero sandwiches and watermelon. When a rock band began to play, the young men and women danced in the streets.

People were intoxicated by the presence of the ships and their crews. The South Street Seaport Museum and the surrounding area remained as boisterous as a carnival. Brass bands played patriotic music, and street vendors hawked everything from horoscopes to teddy bears. City officials, law enforcement personnel, visitors and residents all marveled at the joyous feeling in the streets.

But by July 7, the long pageant was coming to an end. One by one warships, small ships and tall ships began to leave. A few remained another day, but most departed. Some tall ships were scheduled to visit other American cities, others returned to their home ports. After so many days' confinement in the narrow harbor, the sailors were probably glad to unfurl the big ships' sails and head out to the freedom of the sea.

With the majestic visitors gone, New York City returned to a more familiar pace. The Sanitation Department used snowplows to begin clearing away some 1,772 tons of refuse. But the holiday spirit and the arrival of the ships left their mark. As people continued to discuss the amiable crowds and violence-free festival, the city's concept of itself was altered ever so slightly.

Battery Park was 100% humanity as the Fourth of July fireworks display was about to begin.

(Following page) At 9:00 P.M. one of the most lavish displays of fireworks ever produced exploded over New York Harbor. The Statue of Liberty was the center of the pyrotechnics: flares were fired from six locations surrounding the statue.